THE EVERYTHING STORE SALES GUIDE

HOW TO MAKE MONEY WITH AMAZON FBA

BY SMART READS

Free Audiobook

As a thank you for being a Smart Reader you can choose 2 FREE audiobooks from audible.com. Simply sign up for free by visiting www.audibletrial.com/Travis to get your books.

Visit:

www.smartreads.co/freebooks
to receive Smart Reads books for FREE

Check us out on Instagram:

www.instagram.com/smart_readers
@smart_readers

ABOUT SMARTREADS

Choose Smart Reads and get smart every time. Smart Reads sorts through all the best content and condenses the most helpful information into easily digestible chunks.

We design our books to be short, easy to read and highly informative. Leaving you with maximum understanding in the least amount of time.

Smart Reads aims to accelerate the spread of quality information so we've taken the copyright off everything we publish and donate our material directly to the public domain. You can read our uncopyright below.

We believe in paying it forward and donate 5% of our net sales to Pencils of Promise to build schools, train teachers and support child education.

To limit our footprint and restore forests around the globe we are planting a tree for every 10 hardcover books we sell.

Thanks for choosing Smart Reads and helping us help the planet.

Sincerely,

Travis & the Smart Reads Team

Uncopyright 2017 by Smart Reads. No rights reserved worldwide. Any part of this publication may be reproduced or transmitted in any form without the prior written consent of the publisher.

Disclaimer: The publisher and author make no representations or warranties with respect to the accuracy or completeness of these contents and disclaim all warranties for a particular purpose. The author or publisher is not responsible for how you use this information. The fact that an individual or organization is referred to in this document as a citation or source of information does not imply that the author or publisher endorses the information that the individual or organization provided.

TABLE OF CONTENTS

Introduction	2
Chapter 1: Understanding Amazon FBA	4
Chapter 2: How to Create An Amazon FBA Account	7
Chapter 3: What is Arbitrage?	9
Chapter 4: Finding Products To Sell	11
Chapter 5: Creating Private Labels	15
Chapter 6: Restricted Items – What Not To Sell	20
Chapter 7: Creating The Sales Page	21
Chapter 8: Forming a Listing	22
Chapter 9: Shipping Your Products To Amazon	24

Chapter 10: 30
Fees You Need To Know

Chapter 11: 33
Marketing Your Products

Chapter 12: 39
Understanding the Amazon Ranking System

Conclusion 45

Smart Reads Vision 52

INTRODUCTION

Behind the scenes of Amazon, Jeff Bezos, has proved that research pays off, and being in the right place, at the right time, is the key to success. He had read a report, indicating the projected web commerce growth was near 2300%. His initial research led him to create a list of 20 products that could be sold and marketed online.

Think about that for a moment. The man started with 20 products he believed he could sell online.

Founded in 1994, Amazon began as an online bookstore and went online in 1995. Later, the company began to diversify by adding DVDs, CDs, MP3s, streaming downloads, and similar items. The company quickly moved into selling more and more items, eventually becoming the retail giant it is today. But, it's important to remember Bezos didn't become a success overnight.

Profits began to come in during the 4th quarter of 2001 and it has boomed ever since. In 2015, Amazon bypassed Walmart in the United States, as the most valuable retailer. And as of the 3rd quarter of 2016, Amazon is the fourth most valuable public company.

Today, Amazon has separate websites for the US, Ireland, the UK, France, Germany, Canada, Spain, Italy, Netherlands, Brazil, China, Mexico, Canada, India, Japan, and Australia.

Amazon employs an astounding 268,900 people and by opening the doors to third-party sellers, individuals and companies alike, benefit financially.

CHAPTER 1: UNDERSTANDING AMAZON FBA

Have you been looking for a way to start a successful online business? Do you dream of leaving your 9 to 5 job to work for yourself? Would you like to have a position that can give you financial freedom without a ceiling on what you can earn?

If you answered yes to any of these questions, the Fulfillment by Amazon (FBA) may be what you're looking for.

There are countless success stories from people just like you, who truly wanted independence, success, and financial freedom. Guess what? They used FBA to make it happen. So, what exactly is FBA?

If you're familiar with eBay, FBA is fairly similar with many exceptions, one being the auction style. FBA has oodles of tools and resources you won't find anywhere else. Basically, the simplest explanation is this, by buying items that are in demand at huge discounts; you can make HUGE profits with them on Amazon. You operate as a third-party seller on this incredibly large market platform with a ginormous customer base!

Think of it this way, it's like having your own store, and the doors are open in every city, and every country worldwide. The best part, you operate under the protection of this enormous business, but the benefits get better, so keep reading.

With the FBA model, you can send your inventory to one of their many distribution centers for them to handle and ship to your customers. If you're about to ask, "Whoa. Hang on here. You mean I don't have to keep an inventory in my home, garage, or shop?" That's correct!

Of course, if you would like to sell and deal with shipping, returns, and everything that goes along with every transaction, you, of course, can do that. But why would you? Why waste time with tedious and time-consuming tasks, when you could be finding new and exciting stocks to fill your storefront with?

FBA differs in many ways from the basic Amazon seller account. First, the reasons mentioned above, then beyond into the customer service arena. Even better, products that are housed in Amazon's distribution centers qualify for Prime, giving your customers lightning-fast shipping. Do note that your inventory stored in distribution centers will incur storage fees, so it is imperative that you find items that will move quickly. We will cover this in depth in a later section.

FBA is all about research and strategy. There are guidelines you will need to know in order to be successful, and these will be covered as well. First, you will need to buy low and sell high. This is how you will earn money and there are many ways to do this. Local resources can be a viable source of great stock at a cheap price. Sometimes, items you find in your own locale may not be available anywhere else, so don't discount this prospect.

Second, you will have competition and oodles of it. You will have to work diligently at being the best seller you can be. By striving to be the best, you will earn better reviews and in turn, higher listings. Amazon is set up to give the advantage to those who have attained this goal. In order to compete with the best, you need to be the best. This is accomplished by competitive pricing, building credibility, and earning stellar reviews. There is no faster way to move up the ranks.

Third, you will need to utilize technology, such as a cell phone or tablets with apps that will help you stay current with trends, top selling products, and even help you calculate potential profits. You will also need to be fairly savvy with a computer, able to utilize new technologies, and resources.

Fourth, there are two unique ways to sell through Amazon: retail arbitrage and private labeling. Both offer phenomenal profits, but require different approaches to selling.

With research and hard work, you can change your life, your financial status, and your future. Read on and find out more about this amazing opportunity.

CHAPTER 2: HOW TO CREATE AN AMAZON FBA ACCOUNT

You will need an account, but if you already have a seller account, you can simply register, and add FBA to your existing account.

If you are starting from scratch, this is a simple task to complete. Scroll to the bottom of the Amazon main page and find, *"Make Money with Us."* Click on the hyperlink, *"Sell on Amazon."* At this point you can open an individual seller account or register as an FBA seller.

There are many differences between the two types of accounts and these are important to understand. An individual seller account is for sellers that ship less than 40 products a month, but don't start with that type of account just because you're new, and don't believe you'll ship more than that right away. There are significant advantages to a professional seller account.

A professional seller account is able to sell items that are restricted from individual sellers. (We will cover restricted items later). Also, the first month of the professional seller account is free, so why not at least try it out? You can always try it and cancel it before the billing cycle. If you're serious about building your business, you will more than likely want, and need the professional account. **Important**: You can only take advantage of the free month when you sign up.

When you sign up, you will be required to provide credit card information, your name and address and your business name. Hopefully, you have a professional sounding name, or a name that reflects well on your business. You will also have to verify your identity.

A signed participation agreement, obligating you to fulfill Amazon's terms and conditions, will be required of you. A list of guidelines and selling restrictions are included, but you should always stay up-to-date, and check the main website for new restrictions, or changes to existing ones.

Easy. Right? Let's move on to the fun part, figuring out what you want to sell.

CHAPTER 3: WHAT IS ARBITRAGE?

According to Dictionary.com, "arbitrage" in finance, means the *"simultaneous purchase and sale of the same securities, commodities, or foreign exchange in different markets to profit from unequal prices."*

Now that you know the definition, let's explore three main sources: retail, garage sales, and online.

In retail, you will be out scouting for deals, and deeply discounted items. But how do you know if these products will sell? There are many different apps that can assist you with research, inventory management, and also analyzing your profitability. One is the **Amazon Seller** app, and it is available for Android, as well as iOS phones. The app is free with mixed ratings concerning usage. **Inventory Lab** is another app, but will cost you around $49 a month. Depending on your circumstances, the level you end up selling on, only a trial will be able to give you a definitive answer as to which one is better.

Other barcode scanning apps are available, but ultimately, you will need to decide which one works best for you. Apps like **Scoutify** and **Profit Bandit** are multifaceted apps able to calculate profit for a potential product, but they will also factor in all the fees that will be associated with a sale, such as FBA seller fees, and shipping fees. Be aware, many of these apps have a monthly fee to use, but most offer the first 30 days for free.

There is a potential downfall to arbitrage; the time you spend scouting for items, and traveling from store to store or yard sale to yard sale. A lot of energy and dedication is required. The scanning apps mentioned above will help make the task easier, but you must consider the time they have available. With research, organization, and the right app, you could be on your way to financial freedom.

Tip to remember: Avoid items that are not marked down below 50%. Some users encourage you to look for items on clearance for over 70%. Again, scanning apps will give you the data you need to make an informed decision, and hopefully, it's a product that will be profitable.

CHAPTER 4: FINDING PRODUCTS TO SELL

How and where to find products that will make a profit will depend on which direction you want to go. We've talked about arbitrage, but there is another avenue, and it is called private labeling. If you are new to selling online, you may be more comfortable with arbitrage at first. We will cover private labeling later. For now, let's discuss what sells, and where to find them.

First, you will want to know what the best sellers are on Amazon. To accomplish this, simply search, **"Top items sold on Amazon."** You will find an Amazon link to their best sellers' page. This list is updated hourly.

Products are broken up by category, such as, electronics, toys and games, clothes, etc. The top three items will be pictured with a link to see more items. Click on the, **"see more items"** link and you will get the top 100 items being sold in that category. How powerful is that?

The list is broken down further on the sidebar. Let's start with toys and games. As this e-book is being written, the #1 seller for all toys and games is, ***Cards Against Humanity.*** Since the seller is none other than the company that designed it, the odds aren't in your favor for finding this product at a discount, or even competing with them. We'll move on to the second best seller, and it is a fidget cube. They are cheap, under $5, and unless they can be found at $1.50 or less, there would be very little profit to be made. Remember, you need to find items at a discount, 50% or more, and closer to 70% if at all possible.

The first two items weren't very promising, but keep researching. Use this knowledge and keep your eyes open when out shopping for deals. Scan through multiple best seller lists of products you would be either willing to sell, have the ability to find at a discount, or can find similar products that will be competitive.
So, you have a little knowledge of what is selling in toys and games. On your next shopping/researching venture, you might find a sale at a local retail store, say Target. At Target, the card game, Uno, is under clearance for $1. What a deal, right? Or is it?

This is where you will use the technology readily available on your phone. You can go the long route and search for it on Amazon, or if you downloaded a scanning app, you can simply scan the barcode. Remember, many of these apps will calculate your profit minus your seller fees, including shipping.

After scanning, it shows the potential profit for an UNO card is around $3 per deck. Well, that's great and all, but exactly how many will sell on Amazon? Before you get excited, you need to know if you're buying a product that will move quickly, or an item that will just sit in a warehouse, and cost you storage fees. Do your homework. With further research, it turns out, Uno is #14 in toys and games. Score!

Do remember you will have competition, but there's a lot going for this product. First, it is cheap. Second, it is small, meaning that it will take up less space in an Amazon warehouse, and if it doesn't move as quickly as you'd like, storage fees will be minimal. This could be a great payday, but can you make it any better? Do not discount the power of negotiation. At this point, you can clear out the shelf, and be merrily on your way. Or you can contact the manager, and offer to buy say, two or three cases. And if you have the resources, maybe you could offer to buy everything he has for an extra 10% off.

Hey, you can try. But what if the manager accepts? Retail stores continuously rotate stock throughout the seasons. Items come and go. When they need to get rid of items quickly, what do they do? They put them on clearance! This is the gold you will need to be looking for. Don't just buy items that you think will sell. Buy items you know will sell. Amazon charges $0.54 per cubic square feet for standard sized items January-October monthly. Oversized items are $0.43 per cubic square feet.
For the holiday months, November and December, the price increases to $2.25 per cubic square feet for standard items monthly. Oversized items jump to $1.15 per cubic square feet monthly.

What you decide to sell is entirely up to you, but find a niche of similar products, and be competitive. Realize that you will be competing with seasoned veterans, so offer the very best service you can give.

"But I don't have the time to drive all over town searching for items. What now?"
Maybe global trade is for you. The only downfall is the amount of money you will be required to spend upfront. This is why it is so important to research. No one would want to get stuck with a thousand items that aren't selling, not to mention the money spent.

Sites like Alibaba are a great way to find items at huge discounts, but the catch is this, you will be required to buy LOTS of that item in order to get that deal. Pay very close attention to shipping costs and how the company will ship the items. In most cases, companies will ship by sea, air or express (DHL, TNT, USPS, FedEx, EMS).
If you have fully researched a product, and feel confident you can make a profit on it, do not hesitate to contact the company before you order, and get a relatively close shipping estimate. You may find that the great deal isn't so great after all. Maybe the shipping is too expensive and you won't make a profit. These are important variables to consider if you're serious about becoming successful. Research, research, and research some more. Remember, cheap and in demand.

Places to look: Target, Costco, Family Dollar, Dollar Tree, Walgreens, CVS, discount book stores, Sam's Club, Marshall's, Game Stop, outlet malls, TJ Maxx, yard sales, Craigslist, estate sales, and don't forget libraries have book sales too.

CHAPTER 5: CREATING PRIVATE LABELS

When you are ready to take selling on FBA to the next level, private labeling can be a game changer. Similar to retail arbitrage, you will need to do considerable research, and more so with this venture. This is big time. Only serious sellers need apply.
Private labeling is the buying of merchandise from a supplier, labeling with your OWN private label and reselling. With private labeling, you can spend considerably less time searching for more inventory, and more time selling.

You will have to launch your own product line. It is recommended that you first build up the product line first, and obtain reviews, before taking this path. Solid reviews and steady traffic to your products will help launch you into private labeling. Starting from scratch could prove to be a tough endeavor.

When you are ready to dive in, a new world will be opened to you. No longer will you be spending oodles of your time hunting for retail items to resell. In this area of selling, you will only need to find items online, and from big suppliers, like Alibaba, and others.

Note: You will need capital to get started. With money on hand, and an idea, find a niche. Again, it's all about finding a niche, because who wants to sell the same items as thousands of others in an oversaturated market, and compete? The products you consider must be in-demand for you to have any success as well. Start the same way as you did while searching for items in retail arbitrage, find out what's popular, what has high rankings, and use this for every product you consider.

Recommended Products:
• Find items with low weight. Shipping costs are lower, and thus, cost less to ship to you. This will be an important factor.

• Find out who is selling the same or similar items, and study them, compare them. Take into consideration what buyers need to know about a product. Does their listing accurately describe the item? What else could make their listing better? Are there a lot of questions about the product? If so, find out what buyers want to know, and address those when you list your own. Refine your listing by preying on the strengths and weaknesses of others. Hey, you want to make money, right? Research.

• Price your items to earn a reasonable profit, but within a range that it is affordable for buyers. Find items with rankings under 1,000. The closer you move to #1, the stiffer the competition. Stay in an area where you have the ability to come up in search results within the first page or two.

• As mentioned before when using a global supplier, do your homework, and ask them questions before committing to buy. Research the product you want to buy, ensure the quality is good, great is better. Find information about the supplier you plan to buy from.

Sites like Alibaba have ratings for suppliers, read them.

• With private labeling, you will need to look for items that you can resell at 3 times the cost.

• Be sure to read the minimum order quantity. Some require as little as 200, others over 10,000 items. Some sites have tools on the sidebar that allow you to custom search for products within the range you're looking to purchase. This will save you an enormous amount of time.

• Contact the supplier personally and ask for a test batch. Many suppliers are eager for new business and will be happy to do a smaller order. This may save you money. Maybe the product isn't quite what you were looking for. Why get stuck with 1,000, or heaven forbid, 10,000, when 200 would be easier to take?

• Be sure to find out if the products you intent to purchase can be private labeled. Not all can, so be mindful of that fact, and find out.

The research can be tedious, but when you find that perfect product to private label, creativity is your next step. You will need a business logo, right? Packaging? Labels? Maybe you're not creative, you don't have the time, or you simply don't know how. Don't go in it alone. Hire someone. Sites like Upwork, Fiverr, and Freelancer are great places to get you the creative designs you need.

There are a couple of ways to find the perfect freelancer for the job and at a price you set. Let's say you will need the logo first. You want a killer logo that grabs attention. What would that logo be worth? Think about it and then consider the type of freelancer you hope to hire. Do you want a so-so illustrator or a great one? In other words, don't lowball the budget, be fair, consider the time a person will spend creating your logo, and also their knowledge. Set a decent budget and wait for the bids to roll in. Some freelancers will compete for your work and bid considerably lower than your budget. Your job is to pick the candidate you feel would be best to design for you. You can view a freelancer's portfolio, if they have one, and that will make your job a lot easier. Be sure to leave feedback and a review. Freelancers gobble up good reviews like you will, and you both need them to stay competitive.

Design your listing. Create a detailed description of your product. Remember what you learned from product listings from other sellers, and use them to make your listing shine. Well-written product listings do nothing more than up the potential for sales. Be creative and be honest. Use bullet points to set off a series of facts. They're eye-catching, appealing, and professional looking.

Private labeling will cost you more up front over retail arbitrage, but the end result of sales will be significantly better with proper research, and quality products. Don't get discouraged when you begin. Sales may not come in as steady as you'd like at first, but this is the time you need to shine by offering great customer service, and getting much needed reviews to propel your business forward.

CHAPTER 6: RESTRICTED ITEMS – WHAT NOT TO SELL

There are several no-no products when it comes to selling on Amazon. Here are some of them.

- Counterfeit products
- Alcohol, food and beverage, tobacco and drug paraphernalia, skin care items, electronics, services, art, weapons, and make-up

Whoa, wait a minute. People sell make-up and this or that all the time! There are exceptions to some of the above-mentioned products, and you can sell them, but with approval from Amazon to do so. You will also need to have a professional account, offer at least 3 invoices from authorized wholesalers, with a minimum of 200 products. You cannot use retail arbitrage to sell any restricted item.

CHAPTER 7: CREATING THE SALES PAGE

Once you have a professional account, you will have your very own sales page. This page should be professional, visually enticing, and accurately describe your products.

If you haven't thought of a business name yet, be sure to come up with one that is professional sounding, and one that says something about your business.
For keywords, use words that are broad in nature, more likely to come up in searches, but don't put in so many that it will look like spam. You can search for keywords on Amazon in various ways in order to find the ones that best describe your products, or are the most popular.

Amazon has a Keyword Tool in their search bar that auto-completes, showing the most popular searches. Use it to maximize potential traffic. When you add products photos, make sure they are professional-grade, and eye appealing. Taking sloppy pictures with your phone will do nothing more than make you look like an amateur. Your options are to hire to have someone clean up your images, or do it yourself. There are many free photo-imaging sites where you can fix or enhance images. Appearance is very important. Don't work your butt off with everything else and fail now.

CHAPTER 8: FORMING A LISTING

Now that you have a product or products to sell, it is time to create a listing. You will need to first add the items to your inventory before you proceed. On your seller account page, click the **"Inventory"** tab. Next, click, **"Add product."** At this point, you will be required to enter a search term for the item you are selling. You can accomplish this with the name of the product or the barcode.

When you locate the item you are selling, you will proceed to the product information portion of the listing. In this area, you will put in your price, condition of the items, and shipping information. Under shipping, for FBA sellers who will be warehousing their product in an Amazon warehouse, choose, **"I want Amazon to ship and provide customer service for my items if they sell."** This indicates that you will be using the FBA service.

After choosing the option for Amazon to handle shipping and customer service, there is one more important step. Under the **"Inventory"** tab, click on, **"Manage Inventory."** In the drop-down menu, **"Actions,"** select **"Change to Fulfilled by Amazon."**

If you are re-selling used items, such as books, be honest about the condition of the book. Is it fair, good, or nearly new? Don't earn yourself negative feedback by misrepresenting an item. Be vivid in your description. Make your product and yourself as a seller shine with engaging content. Be different. Be unique.

CHAPTER 9: SHIPPING YOUR PRODUCTS TO AMAZON

With Amazon FBA, they are responsible for delivery, but you are responsible for packaging. There are strict guidelines and requirements for packaging. Be sure to learn them and avoid having your entire shipment returned and at your cost.

Keep in mind that all of your products may not go to the same warehouse. There are various reasons for this. Efficient shipping is the biggest reason. Another reason may be that some warehouses are better equipped to handle and store certain or special items.

List of items you need:
- Computer
- Laser or thermal printer (Ink jet printers smear barcodes. Scanners must be able to scan.)
- Labels
- Boxes that adhere to Amazon regulations
- Measuring tape
- Shipping tape
- Bags of appropriate size for your products
- Scale to weigh products
- Smartphone
- Optional in retail arbitrage: price-tag peeler

These items, minus the smartphone, can be found, and purchased through Amazon's Warehouse Network.

Labeling

Everything you send to Amazon must have a barcode. They rely on barcodes. The only way for them to know the product is yours is with proper labeling. You can print Amazon labels from your Amazon seller account. After you select the option to **"Fulfill by Amazon..."** you will be given two labeling options.

FBA Labeling Service
Amazon will label your inventory for you, for a fee, of course. Don't discount this service as your business grows. Time could become an issue, especially if you'll be dealing with hundreds, or even thousands of items. When purchasing large shipments from manufacturers, you may find pricing reasonable to have them label your products, and ship directly to an Amazon warehouse, rather than shipping to you, for you to label, and then ship again. It's all about time and money. Find the best possible solution for every product you stock. Some items can be sent using the manufacturer's barcode. You should check on Amazon's website before using this process.

The following codes are eligible: UPC (Universal Product Code), ISBN (International Standard Book Number), GTIN (Global Trade Item Number), EAN (International/European Article Number), or JAN (Japanese Article Number).

Another option is sticker less/commingling inventory. This option is for new items only. Your items will be added to other sellers' items that are selling the same thing. When your item is purchased, the item will be taken from the commingled stock. The advantage of commingling is faster shipping. Some sellers advise to steer clear from this option, citing that labeling is worth the effort in terms of profit. Only certain items are eligible for commingling to begin with, but it is available if you would like to learn more about it.

Creating a Shipment
1. Inside your seller account, go to Manage Inventory. Once there, choose the item you will ship, and choose Send/Replenish Inventory.

2. Enter the relevant information about the item. This includes: where you are shipping from, the amount, and any restrictions the items may have.

3. Check over the Prepare Products section to find out what preparations you need to make before sending to an Amazon warehouse. You have the option to request that Amazon prepare your items for sale, but this option will carry a fee for the service. Also, there are items that are not eligible for the service.

4. To label your items, you need to decide if you are commingling, or will label your items.

5. After all the information is completed, you may print the labels from the Label Products page or Manage Inventory page, and affix to your items.

6. When all labeling is complete, you will be directed to the Preview Shipments page. There, you will be notified if your items have been split up into different shipments.

7. The final step in this process is to select "Work on Shipment."

How to ship items to Amazon
There are several different options, depending the weight, and size of your shipment. There are two main types of shipping:

• Small parcel delivery (SPD)
• Less-than-truckload (LTL) For shipments over 150 pounds

Shipping is based on distance of travel and weight. Depending on your location, and which Amazon warehouse you will need to ship to, it will be important to get estimates on shipping before deciding which carrier to use.
By using an Amazon-partnered carrier, you can save a lot of work, and can easily track the package while in transit. For SPDs, UPS is the only partner with Amazon at the moment, but be sure to check, and stay informed about partner carriers through Amazon. Once you enter the number of boxes in your shipment, you will print your labels, and affix to shipping boxes.

Printing Amazon Labels
In order for your products to be linked to your seller account, you will need to print labels with Amazon barcodes. You want to get paid, right?

Every item must have an Amazon label. It is recommended to use a laser or thermal printer. Inkjet printers tend to smear ink, so they are highly discouraged. When you affix your label to the item, cover the original product label to avoid confusion. Amazon has different label sizing requirements for the label you will need to use. You should be able to print labels without having to resize them.

The Amazon labels are your basic lifeline to your products in the warehouse. The Fulfillment Network Stock Keeping Unit (FNSKU) is a code for your seller account. The code also relates to the specific Amazon Standard Identification Number (ASIN), which is assigned to every item that Amazon sells. Along with the nifty code for associates to scan, which is important to get paid, included on the labels are the name of the product, and the condition of the product you declared.

Whew, and we haven't even began to put the items into a box! While the prep work may seem tedious, it is extremely important to follow each, and every step. Do not wind up getting your shipment declined because you forgot a step, or worse, the most important label assigning you as the seller.

Packaging Your Items
Note: If your items are not properly packaged, you will be charged a fee.

Important packaging requirements:
• Fragile items require bubble wrap so they won't break if dropped.

- Cloth items or clothes, liquids, toys and children's items, powdered or small grained material, all must be placed in a sealed plastic bag with a suffocation warning.
- Gold or gold sets must be packaged in shrink-wrap, and further packaged into a bag, or box, with a sticker that indicates the complete set is there.
- Amazon can package your items if they have a Universal Product Code (UPC). This service comes with a fee.
- All shipments to an Amazon warehouse cannot be more than 25 inches on any side.
- There are also weight restrictions. Refer to Amazon Shipping and Routing Requirements often, because the restrictions can change.
- Again, if any of the shipment fails to meet Amazon's requirements, the shipment will be returned to you, at your cost.

Once you decide on a carrier, and your shipment is on its way, you are not officially off the hook until the shipment arrives at the specified Amazon warehouse. Keep tracking information and ensure your shipment arrives, and is delivered on time.

Any discrepancies, damage, or missing items will be reported to you. In the event this happens, you will need to speak with Amazon regarding reimbursement, or the fees you'll be charged for the return shipment. It may be advisable to insure your shipment with the shipping carrier before departure.

CHAPTER 10: FBA FEES YOU NEED TO KNOW

Amazon FBA isn't free, but the exposure, and opportunity to sell to millions is worth it. Make sure to note that fees constantly change, usually around the change of financial quarters.

There are two different types of fees, and they are based on which fulfillment type you are using. Amazon fulfillment is strictly for Amazon. There is another type of fulfillment that is pretty awesome for those who sell on other sites, such as Etsy, and eBay. We will cover Multi-Channel selling in a later section.

Fee Types
You will be charged a fee based on the handling, packing, and weight of your items shipped to customers, called Pick and Pack. Fees vary from item to item, such as; oversized, Media, Non-Media items, and by product type. If you're feeling overloaded, take a deep breath, because you have so much more to learn. The great thing though is that if you are selling an item worth over $300.00, you can sell it without fees being leveraged against it.

You do not have to calculate the fees associated with the sale of your items. Amazon has the FBA Revenue Calculator on hand. All you need to do is input specific information. Once calculated, you will get a potential earning for the item, giving you a relatively accurate bottom line.

Information you will be required to enter:
- Item price
- Shipping – by using the FBA, Amazon takes over the cost, so this cost is 0.
- Order handling – this could be a flat rate or a fee that is determined by the type of item it is.
- Pick and pack – this fee refers to the cost you incurred by shipping the items to the warehouse, unless you improperly packaged the items. If so, you will be charged a fee for the item to be packaged properly.
- Weight handling – this fee is calculated by an Amazon scale. There are special fees for certain items, like televisions, or other large, and awkward items.
- Monthly storage – you will be charged per cubic square feet of volume for the space your items take up in the warehouse. This fee is figured monthly and differs based on your stock.
- Inbound shipping – this figure is the charges you incurred shipping your items to an Amazon warehouse.
- Customer service – the cost of customer service is already included in a professional seller account. No extra charge in this category.
- Prep service – this only applies if you request Amazon prep your items. The fee is calculated per item.

Storage Fees
Since Amazon charges storage fees, it is extremely important to choose carefully when selecting items to sell. You will want items that will sell quickly and

move out of the warehouse as soon as possible. Don't fill up the warehouse with Christmas decorations in February. This sounds like a no-brainer, but this is the type of situation you need to avoid. Gear your stock, if seasonal, for the appropriate season. Storage is more expensive in the last half of the year for the holiday shopping season.

If the items in your inventory sell slowly, and end up in storage for over six months, you will need to pay a long-term fee, and this varies, depending on the items. The long-term fee only works for bulk items, not single items.

When initially choosing between an individual selling plan and a professional selling plan, it is important to note that an extra $0.99 is charged against your item in return for FBA service. With a professional selling account, you keep that money.
Inventory dates for Amazon are August 15th and February 15th. Use these dates as a guide when you plan to restock.

CHAPTER 11: MARKETING YOUR PRODUCTS

Since Amazon is basically a huge search engine, the best way to improve sales is by getting them to come up earlier in the search results.

Keywords are everything on Amazon. When you list items on Amazon, you will have a field to enter your keywords. These are words and phrases customers use to search for products, and hopefully get directed to your doorstep. This is why it is so important to utilize the best keywords for your item when listing. You want customers to be directed toward your products, right?

Let's say you have a coffee maker to sell. To help illustrate this point, follow along on Amazon. There are a number of important keywords here. Consider the many ways a customer might search for a coffee maker. They may use "coffee maker." That's a pretty broad search with over 50k products, but a basic keyword to use. On the left sidebar, the results are broken down even further because there are lots of types of coffee makers. What type of coffee maker are you selling? Is it an espresso coffee maker? A single-serve coffee maker? Is it a combo brew type machine? These are important questions to answer in the keywords.

If you're following along, you might have noticed the keyword, "coffee machine" came up as well. People use many different terms, depending on the region they are from. Understand this and use it to your advantage. While you're at it, add coffee machine to your keywords.

We have a basic coffee maker/machine. No espresso, no single-serve. It's just an add water and coffee ground, and push start model. What brand it is? Put the brand name in the keywords. Now, what model is it? Again, dissect exactly what this coffee maker is, and use those keywords. Is it programmable? How many cups does it make? As you can see, we are narrowing down the search for customers who are looking for the product we have.

By the way, there were only 83 of the above-mentioned coffee makers. Again, it's all about describing your product with accurate keywords.

Tip: Don't forget that people misspell words when searching for items. Is it coffeemaker or coffee maker?

Get Feedback from Buyers!
The statistic is that nearly 90% of buyers on Amazon do not leave feedback after a purchase. As a newbie, you will need great feedback, and lots of it in order to propel your sales, and get noticed.

The best way is to offer incentives to customers for leaving a review. This could be a coupon for a free product or a discount. While this will cost you some money early on, this can lead to repeat customers, and more sales. Remember, good feedback and reviews, are GOLD.

Tip: Do an online search for coupon companies seeking Amazon product coupons. Use promo codes to entice buyers to your doorstep.

Amazon Pay-Per-Click Advertising
There are two ways to get noticed on Amazon. When a person comes to Amazon, most of the time, they know exactly what they are looking for. Their search, which will generally be three words, will produce two kinds of relevant results.

Organic results: results for a search where sellers with good ratings, and reviews, are at the top.
Paid results: results that are paid advertising. These often times come up before organic results.

If you don't have a lot of feedback or reviews, paying for pay-per-click advertising may be a good idea to jumpstart your business, or improve what you already have.
Pay-per-click isn't worth a dime if you don't understand the basics of keywords, and utilize the best ones for your product. There is more to this service than simply submitting your listing. You want to get the most for your money, don't you?

Create a Campaign
Go to Amazon Services to make your product a Sponsored Product. Management of advertising is utilized through Seller Central in the Advertising

section. Ads are broken up into different campaigns, if you are advertising more than one item. Start a campaign by choosing a name for your advertising program. This is only visible to you and you can change it later if you like. You will need to input various information about your campaign. Budget will be important and you will need to decide on an amount for the entire campaign. Break this down into a daily budget. Many sellers recommend $50 to $80 a day. Your budget is entirely up to you. The figure is only a maximum of what you're "willing" to spend, not what you will spend.

Amazon's Buy Box
You cannot buy the Buy Box. You have to earn it. But what is it? And why should you want it? The Buy Box is the little blue box on the right side of a seller's listing with the "Add to Cart" button. This is golden real estate for Amazon sellers. Customers can buy a product with a simple click. Sellers with a Buy Box gain placement advantages for their products as well.

- Only professional sellers on Amazon can win the Buy Box.
- Only one merchant per product will win the Buy Box.

Amazon consistently pushes for the very best customer service and shopping experience. As a seller, you must meet certain performance-based requirements in order to win the Buy Box. Amazon does not disclose the unique recipe, much like Colonel Sanders, but they do admit that excelling in all areas enhances a seller's chances of winning the box.

- Pricing – be competitive. Watch your competition and find out who is consistently winning the buy box.
- Availability – keep your products in stock at all times, especially popular items. No stock for an item = no buy box eligibility, and more than likely, negative feedback from a customers.
- Fulfillment – offer multiple shipping options, including free shipping.
- Customer Service – respond to questions from customers as soon as possible. Follow up transactions with a thank you email.
- Product Listing – list your products accurately with a proper title, description, condition, and category.
- Order Defect Rate (ODR) – the rate of returns, chargebacks, and customer claims. Another reason to only sell high quality items.
- Seller Status – the length of time you have been selling on Amazon also plays a factor in the matrix, but don't allow this to discourage you. Sellers with the Buy Box have significantly more sales. If you don't win the buy box, you could still earn a spot in the, "Other Buying Options" section below the buy box.

Tip: Bundle products to create unique items.

Multi-Channel Fulfillment
Multi-Channel Fulfillment enables you, as a seller, to fill orders from other sites, such as eBay, using your inventory that is stored in an Amazon warehouse. This is great news for those of you already selling on eBay. The time saved on shipping activities could be phenomenal.

To request a product to be fulfilled to a non-Amazon customer, use the "Amazon Fulfills web form." Fill out the form with your buyer's name and address, and pertinent shipping instructions. You can even add a customized note to the buyer on the packing slip.

Note: Amazon will charge you for the shipping fees.

Why should I sell on Amazon and eBay?
• Both are still growing. Amazon attracts 20 million customers a month. eBay follows with 15 million visitors a month.
• While customers to both sites may overlap, they each have their own user base. To reach the most customers, using both greatly expands your potential sales.

CHAPTER 12: UNDERSTADING THE AMAZON RANKING SYSTEM

We barely scratched the surface of ranking. In a previous section, we happened upon playing cards that were ranking #14 in toys and games. But what does that really mean? And out of how many? Number 14 would be completely different in another category, say a folk music LP. How many people could possibly be buying those? Maybe more than you think. Who knows?

For retail arbitrage, the recommendation for buying items to sell need to have a ranking lower than 50,000. Lower is better. For instance, Amazon sells around 480 million different items, with new items being added daily. Think about that for a moment. Think some more. That's a crazy amount of items! Now, where would you like the items you'll be selling to rank? In the top million? Top half a million?
No, we want items that sell, and sell quickly. Amazon is global. Consider all the people buying on their platform every day. We can begin to see why we need to buy items with rankings lower than 50k.

Statistics:
- There were 244 million active users on Amazon as of May 2014
- There were 54 million Amazon Prime users as of January 2016
- 44% of households in the US have Amazon Prime as of September 2016

- Amazon 2016 third quarter net sales was $32.7 billion
- Amazon 2016 third quarter net income was $252 million
- The percentage of web shoppers that go to Amazon first was 44% as of October 2015

If you read through those statistics and reread points four and five a couple of times, you must have asked yourself, where did the 32.4 billion go between the two figures? Much of that money goes to third-party sellers.

Register Your Business
Here we are, at the no so fun side. Many do not realize that by signing up with FBA they are required to pay taxes. In order to pay the taxes you will be liable for, you must first register your business.

You can register your business under your name. If you don't want to use your personal name, you will need to have a "Doing Business As (DBA)" name. A DBA is needed for sole proprietorships and limited liability companies.

Depending on which state you reside in, the laws, and regulations may differ.
As a sole proprietor, your overhead costs are lower, but you may have extra risks. Everything you have is on the line as a sole proprietor, meaning if you get sued for a faulty product, your home, car, you name it, can be taken if need be, to satisfy the debt.

With a Limited Liability Company (LLC), you would have protection from claims that you would not as a sole-proprietor, but your taxes will be different. There are two types of LLCs for you to choose from. If you are an independent owner, you can opt for a single-member LLC, and be treated the same legally as a sole proprietor. If you have a partner or partners, there is a Multi-partner LLC. These types of entities vary from state to state, so it is up to you to learn about what is best for you, and your business.

Federal Taxes
Your FBA business is a form of self-employment, according to law. You will also need to file paperwork for Self-Employment tax in order to pay your income tax, Medicare on salaried income, and Social Security taxes. The amount you will be required to pay is based on the income you earn. Whoa. Hold on a second! I just want to sell items on Amazon!

Small businesses making over $400 a year in profit are required to file a Form 1040. Amazon reports on a quarterly basis, so you will have to collect your tax information quarterly as well. Do not get yourself in a mess legally by skipping this step. In order to have a successful business, you need to complete even the most unsavory of tasks, taxes being one of them.

Taxpayer Identification Number (TIN)
Once you receive a taxpayer identification number, realize that the number is not a business license. While your social security number would work, a TIN is highly recommended. Plus, the advantage of having

a TIN could lend to being taken more seriously by wholesale companies, especially when negotiating.

Collecting Sales Tax

Once you have registered with your state's tax board, you can begin to collect taxes on the products you sell.

Amazon FBA may make running your business easier in many ways, but tax collection gets more complicated, because you will be using Amazon's warehouses in multiple states. This is termed as a multiple state nexus. Before you give up, or get a headache, do note that regulations are somewhat in limbo over online businesses regarding state tax. You will need to stay up to date with new regulations or requirements.

With the exception of 5 states, every other state in the U.S. has some form of requirement for taxation and collection of taxes. Depending on which state your products end up being stored in, you will be required to collect taxes on those items as well. You will need to find out which states your products are in, and then apply for permits in those states to collect sales tax on the items you sell.

How to find the information you will need:

In your Amazon reports, under your Seller Central page, go to the Inventory tab, and select Inventory Event Detail. You can download this report. Every warehouse your items are stored in will have an ID number. The three-letter number is under the column labeled, fulfillment-cent-id. After the three-letter code, there will be either a 1, 2, or 3.

The first three letters indicate the closest airport to the Amazon warehouse, thereby the state your items are in. You can use the airport codes listed in your Amazon report to help you.

Collecting taxes where you have a sales nexus:
Once you know which states your products are stored in, you will need to apply for a sales tax permit for those particular states. As mentioned before, each state has different requirements. Many states do not charge a fee for registering your business, and collecting sales tax, but some will.

Tax Collecting Services
There are services you can utilize that will establish your tax needs and handle the rest for you, for a fee. There are also websites that have guides for registering in every state. Outside of guides to aid you, they offer services to handle your taxes as well. Before you jump in, and allow someone else to do this unsavory work, you are advised to consult a lawyer.

Amazon offers services for Professional Sellers regarding taxes and tax collection. This service is fee based. Dealing with multiple states in the nexus would be complicated at best; therefore it may be worth it to you to pay for the service. Do realize that with Amazon's service, you are still required to calculate the refunds yourself.

Important to Remember:
Keep detailed records of your income and expenses. This includes fuel spent to acquire items to sell, the cost of shipping products, and basically anything that costs you money to run your FBA business. Consult a tax advisor for a complete list. Don't miss any deductions, because the more you have, the lower your income will appear, and therefore, the taxes owed by you will be lower.

CONCLUSION

Hopefully, after reading this guide to Amazon FBA, you have gained enough information to start your own FBA business. Many people, just like you, were in the same position once, and are now using Amazon as their main income source.

The Amazon platform offers an amazing opportunity with an enormous customer base worldwide. By shipping your products to an Amazon fulfillment warehouse, you will be saving an outrageous amount of time, and resources.

Remember, FBA is all about research and strategy. You will have to buy low and sell high in order to make money. Don't forget there may be items in your locale that aren't available anywhere else, so don't discount what's at your doorstep. To sell more and earn more, you will need to be the best seller that you can be. Earn great reviews, price competitively, and build credibility with every product sold.

You can pursue a couple of different avenues in order to make money on Amazon. First with retail arbitrage, and the other with private labeling. Either one will change your financial circumstances, but it will be ultimately up to you to decide what is best for your situation.

Tip to remember:

Avoid items that are not marked down below 50%. It is better to find items marked down for at least 70% or more.

With private labeling, find items that you can resell at 3 times the cost.

Creating an FBA account is a simple task. There are two different types of accounts; an individual seller account, or the professional seller account. The individual account is geared toward sellers who sell less than 40 items per month, but don't get discouraged, and not give the professional seller account a try.

Note: Remember, you can only take advantage of the free month of the professional seller service when you first sign up.

Take advantage of, and utilize apps that will help you make important decisions concerning products you're considering. You can get the Amazon Seller app for Android and iOS phones. Other apps are out there, but some charge monthly, so be sure to consider what you need before handing over your hard earned money.

In the retail arbitrage area, find deeply discounted deals, and don't hesitate to speak to a store manager about buying more than what is on the shelf. Remember, stores clearance items in order to move them out. Make the most of the deal and negotiate. Retail stores and places to consider: Target, Costco, Family Dollar, Dollar Tree, Walgreens, CVS, discount book stores, Sam's Club, Marshall's, Game Stop, outlet malls, TJ Maxx, yard sales, Craigslist, estate sales, and even libraries.

Be aware of the fees associated with selling your products. The Amazon Seller app or similar seller apps will help you make good decisions when choosing products to sell.

Things to consider when buying items: weight, size, and how fast those items will sell. Again, Amazon charges storage fees, so only purchase items that will move quickly. Also, keep in mind items that are forbidden or restricted. If global trade and buying in bulk is something you're interested in pursuing, be sure to research not only the product, but the company as well. Take into consideration the minimum order required and contact them for an estimated shipping cost. A good deal might be a very bad deal if the shipping is too costly.

After you have properly labeled and packaged your items for sale, double-check your work to ensure the shipment meets Amazon's requirements. Don't miss a step and end up having your shipment returned.

When you create your sales page, keep it professional, and eye-catching. If you need a logo created, you can hire someone to do it for you. Be sure to check sites like Fiverr, Upwork, and Freelancer.

While creating listings for you products, make them stand out with great descriptions, and images. Use bullet points to highlight facts about the product. Visit successful sellers' stores and check out their sales pages. Go the extra mile, make your products shine, encourage reviews, and answer customer questions in a timely manner.

Tip: Offer a discount to customers who leave a review for their next visit.
Market you items properly with the right keywords. Use commonly misspelled words as keywords as well. Include important information about your products; model numbers, brand name, and other key selling points.

Know that you will have competition and you must stay ahead of your competitors. You can achieve this by utilizing the best keywords for your products, by creating better, and more informative listings. Remember, bullet points will help dissect your information, and they are also professional looking.

Work toward earning the Buy Box for your products. Only professional sellers can earn the box, so keep this in mind when choosing what type of seller account you choose. Sellers who earn the Buy Box for their products enjoy more sales.

Tip: Bundle products to create unique items and earn that Buy Box!

Don't forget that you can utilize Multi-Channel Fulfillment. Your reach and potential sales will increase exponentially. Amazon attracts 20 million customers a month. eBay follows with 15 million. Each platform has their own unique user base, so do yourself a favor, and open your doors up to a bigger audience.

Do your homework ahead of time concerning your business by registering a business name. Your FBA business is a form of self-employment and any small business earning over $400 a year is required to file a Form 1040. You will also need to file paperwork for Self-employment tax in order to pay income taxes.

While dealing with taxes and paying Uncle Sam ranks the lowest as far as fun, it is required, and will save you a headache later if you do it right to begin with. Keep detailed records of your income and expenses. Consult a tax advisor for a complete list of deductions, and with any questions you may have.

Realize that you are working and investing in yourself. Set goals that are reasonable and work towards attaining them. Set more goals and keep yourself motivated. Amazon FBA is not a get rich quick scheme. It is a business that will require a lot of hard work.

Tip: Find your niche.

With careful planning, research, and a lot of hard work, you too can enjoy the financial benefits of having your own business. The sky is the limit on what you can earn.

THANKS FOR READING

We really hope you enjoyed this book. If you found this material helpful feel free to share it with friends. You can also help others find it by leaving a review where you purchased the book. Your feedback will help us continue to write books you love.

The Smart Reads library is growing by the day! Make sure and check out the other wonderful books in our catalog. We would love to hear which books are your favorite.

Visit:
www.smartreads.co/freebooks
to receive Smart Reads books for FREE

Check us out on Instagram:
www.instagram.com/smart_readers
@smart_readers

Don't forget your 2 FREE audiobooks.
Use this link www.audibletrial.com/Travis to claim your 2 FREE Books.

SMART READS ORIGINS

Smart Reads was born out of the desire to find the best information fast without having to wade through the sheer volume of fluff available online. Smart Reads combs through massive amounts of knowledge compiles the best into quick to read books on a variety of subjects.

We consider ourselves Smart Readers, not dummies. We know reading is smart. We're self taught. We like to learn a TON about a WIDE variety of topics. We have developed a love for books and we find intelligence attractive.

We found that each new topic we tried to learn about started with the challenge of finding the pieces of the puzzle that mattered most. It becomes a treasure hunt rather than an education.

Smart Reads wants to find the best of the best information for you. To condense it into a package that you can consume in an hour or less. So you can read more books about more topics in less time.

OUR MISSION

Smart Reads aims to accelerate the availability of useful information and will publish a high quality book on every major topic on amazon.

Smart Reads hopes to remove barriers to sharing by taking the copyright off everything we publish and donating it to the public domain. We hope other publishers and authors will follow our example.

Our goal is to donate $1,000,000 or more by 2020 to build over 2,000 schools by giving 5% of our net profit to Pencils of Promise.

We want to restore forests around the globe by planting a tree for every 10 physical books we sell and hope to plant over 100,000 trees by 2020.

Doesn't it feel good knowing that by educating yourself you are helping the world be a better place? We think so too…

Thanks for helping us help the world. You Smart Reader you…

Travis and the Smart Reads Team

WHY I STARTED SMART READS

Every time I wanted to learn about something new I'd have to buy 20 books on the topic and spend way too long sorting through them and reading them all until I arrived at the big picture. Until I had enough perspectives to know who was just guessing, who was uninformed and who had stumbled upon something remarkable.

I wished someone else could just go in and figure that out for me and tell me what matters. That's how smart reads was born. I want smart reads to be a company that does all that research up front. Sorts through all the content that is available on each topic and pulls out the most up to date complete understanding, then have people smarter than me package the best wisdom in an easy to understand way in the least amount of words possible.

For example, I got a new puppy so I wanted to learn about dog training. I bought 14 different books about dog training and by the time I got through the first 5 and finally started getting the big picture on the best way to train my puppy she had grown up into a dog.

Yeah she's well behaved. She doesn't poop in the house. I can get her to sit and come when I call. But what if someone else went in and read all those books for me, found the underlying themes and picked out the best information that would give me the big picture and get me right to the point. And I'd only have to read one book instead of 15.

That would be amazing. I would save time. And maybe my dog would be rolling over, cleaning up after my kids and doing the dishes by now. That my friend, is the reason I started smart reads. Because I wanted a company I can trust to deliver me the best information in an easy to understand way that I can digest in under an hour. Because dog training is one of many subjects I want to master.

The quicker I can learn a wide variety of topics the sooner that information can begin playing a role in shaping my future. And none of us knows how long that future will be. So why not do everything we can to make the best of it and consume a ton of knowledge. And I figured all the better if I can also make a positive difference in the world.

That's why we're also building schools, planting trees and challenging ideas about copyright's place in today's world. Because as a company we have to be doing everything we can to support the ecosystem that gives us all these beautiful places to read our books. Thanks for reading.

Travis

Customers Who Bought This Book Also Bought

Understanding Affiliate Marketing: An Internet Marketing Guide for How To Make Money Online Using Products, Websites and Services

Success Principles: Techniques for Positive Thinking, Self Love and Developing a Powerful

Credit Repair Guide: How to Fix Credit Score and Remove Negatives From Credit Report

Self-Esteem Supercharger: Build Self Worth and Find Your Inner Confidence

Blockchain Revolution: Understanding the Internet of Money

Neuro Linguistic Programming: NLP Techniques for Hypnosis, Mind Control, Human Behavior, Relationships, Confidence

Blockchain Revolution: Understanding the Internet of Money

Passive Income: Do What You Want When You Want and Make Money While You Sleep